by each other's faith.

ROMANS 1:12

JOB & CAREER
Men at Work

Gary Wilde, ed.

A DIVISION OF SCRIPTURE PRESS PUBLICATIONS INC.
USA CANADA ENGLAND

Scripture quotations are from the *Holy Bible, New International Version®*. Copyright © 1973, 1978, 1984 by International Bible Society. Used by permission of Zondervan Publishing House. All rights reserved.

Editors: Carolyn Nystrom & Greg Clouse
Designer: Andrea Boven
Cover Illustration: Mark Stearney
Cartoons: Rob Portlock

Recommended Dewey Decimal Classification: 248.832
Suggested Subject Heading: PERSONAL RELIGION, MEN

ISBN: 1-56476-478-8

1 2 3 4 5 6 7 8 9 10 Printing/Year 00 99 98 97 96

©1996 by Victor Books/SP Publications, Inc.
All rights reserved. Printed in the United States of America.

No part of this book may be reproduced without written permission, except for brief quotations in books and critical reviews. For information write Victor Books, 1825 College Avenue, Wheaton, IL 60187.

Table of Contents

Introduction

Session 1: Dedicated . . . or Just Busy? ▸ 11

Session 2: Success . . . or Failure? ▸ 19

Session 3: Fame . . . or Family? ▸ 25

Session 4: Quit . . . or Stick with It? ▸ 31

Session 5: Knuckle Under . . . or Blow the Whistle? ▸ 38

Session 6: Contentment . . . or "Life Engineering"? ▸ 46

Group Strengtheners

Creative Session Starters ▸ 53

Fellowship Day Idea Starter ▸ 58

Video Night Discussion Outline ▸ 59

Prayer Record ▸ 63

Notes

John opened up a 24-hour store 5 years ago.
That was the last time we saw him.

Introduction

Welcome to...

An exciting men's study experience! Whether you'll be meeting with others in a group, or just going through this book on your own, you've made an excellent decision by choosing *Encouragers for Men*.

The volumes in this series are for men from every background and denomination, men who typically meet together to share their joys and hardships, their life concerns and prayer needs, their spiritual insights and questions—in short, to share their lives. Groups usually meet at lunch break or during an early morning breakfast. Or they may meet in a home during the evening.

According to a popular men's movement, our society views men as mostly self-reliant, unable to feel or express emotion, unconcerned about fellowship, using people but loving things, primarily competitive, and too macho. You are taking an important step toward changing that situation.

Why This Topic?

Many men long for a group in which they can safely reveal their problems and receive the support they need to overcome them. Finding and befriending a fellow struggler brings tremendous encouragement, as men discover that they are not alone.

The book you've chosen, *Job and Career: Men at Work*, emphasizes the importance of this kind of fellowship for men who wish to explore career issues, such as:

- the tensions between career dedication and kingdom commitment
- struggling with feelings of failure
- giving up a dream or career goal because of family needs
- feeling bored or unappreciated at work
- struggling with career-change decisions
- being aware of unethical practices at work
- learning contentment in a world bent on hoarding

What happens when men do *not* find a group where this kind of sharing takes place? They may bog down in their spiritual journeys in one of two ways. First, some men continue seeking to control their circumstances. This stance characterizes the man who says, "I believe I should be joyful; I should feel fulfilled. But I never seem to reach it. I try and try, but something always goes wrong." When faced with dissatisfaction in life, he tries to force the circumstances to change so that he can once again feel happy. It doesn't work.

Second, some men keep trying to "act the part." This is almost the opposite approach. These are the guys who try to act as though things really are working out great all the time. Not content to savor the blessings and joys God sprinkles into their years, they may pretend unbroken daily bliss. In effect, they begin to fake the Christian life, wearing the mask of continual victory. And of course that doesn't work for long either.

The third and more truly Christian approach to life is left to those who are learning to embrace the pain – the pain and the struggle of spiritual pilgrimage. It's not the easy route to take, but it is the most honest. It brings us down to a basic reality, that everything we are and have is a product of the pure, unconditional grace of our Heavenly Father. And here's the key point: This approach to Christian living cannot be done in a vacuum. It requires fellowship, mutual encouragement, and ongoing accountability as men meet together to discuss their progress (successes and failures) along with their need for prayer. That is the way they help each other live for God, all along the way to Christian maturity.

How to Use This Guide

For Individual Use
Any man can benefit from personal study of the stories, Bible passages, quotes, and questions in this book. Just set aside a few minutes each day to be alone and in silence with your Lord. Ask Him to show you what you need to be learning about fellowship in His church. When you come to statements that refer to a group, creatively adapt them to your own relationship with God or with people that you know. Then try to put some of your insights into practical action.

For Use in a Men's Group
These sessions work great in a group of three to ten men. Make sure every man has a book, and use rotating leadership each week. Participants should try to come to the session having read the chapter.

But for those who come unprepared, the chapters are short enough to skim or read aloud during the group time itself. The key to the study format is simply "laying material out on the table" for discussion. Men will pick up on this and feel free to let the discussion move into their particular areas of concern.

Preparing to Lead a Group Session

See the *Can You Relate?* section of each session for your basic outline as you take your turn leading discussion in the group. When it's your turn to lead, your job is to act as a discussion facilitator, not a teacher. Before the session you'll spend some time thinking about how the readings relate to your own journey of spiritual growth. Answer the three questions below, and you will have all the material you need for generating discussion—because people will feel free to contribute their own insights, comments, and questions in response. (You will also find specific questions about your particular topic in the section, *For Further Thought or Discussion*.)

- What experience in your own life confirms (or disputes) the material you've read?
- What themes or statements stand out to you as most important, significant, or controversial?
- What questions, comments, insights, or personal applications flow from this material?

Getting a Handle on the Format

Here are some explanations of the items you'll find in each *Encouragers* chapter. Items 2, 3, and 4 below provide the overall theme for discussion. Group members will choose the parts of these story-sections that strike them as significant, and they'll relate those

INTRODUCTION

stories to their own experience. The goal is personal application, in the context of group accountability, for the purpose of solid spiritual growth.

▶ 1. *Check-In/Update.* Sessions typically open with each group member "reporting in." Sharing consists of "I" statements about life as it is at the moment: A feeling to report, a problem to share, a personal or spiritual growth question/insight, a summary of the week, a progress/accountability check.

▶ 2. *One Man's Story.* This opening vignette offers one man's experience with the topic. It is a personal, "how-I-see-this-issue" report, intended to put the subject into the context of everyday life.

▶ 3. *God Enters the Story.* These are printed Scripture passages related to the topic—there for your reference. Some groups will focus heavily here, others will simply let the Scripture serve as a theological boundary for the discussion. The fact is that "our story" (the way we actually live) often clashes with God's story (the call to deeper commitment and holiness). This creates a tension that makes for excellent discussion: How can God's story become, to a greater degree, the story of our own Christian growth?

▶ 4. *The Story in Quotes.* These brief excerpts add spice to your discussion. They are sometimes profound insights, sometimes controversial thought-starters. Some group members will agree with the statements, others may disagree. The quotes are often drawn from the devotional classics, but can come from any source, secular or religious.

▶ 5. *Can You Relate?* You'll find a set of four general questions in each session. The leader uses these questions to make up the basic "plan" of the session time. Sometimes your group will go no further than responding to these questions.

▶ 6. *For Further Thought or Discussion.* Here you will find creative ways to explore the issues raised in this particular chapter.

▶ 7. *Prayer Moments.* Your group members will choose, each week, how to use their prayer time. Varying the approach gives each group member a chance to pray in a way that is most comfortable.

▶ 8. *Suggestion for the Week Ahead.* Here you're given practical life-response suggestions related to the week's topic. You may wish to use these suggestions to set up an ongoing accountability report to be given during each session. This is a way of inviting each other to check up on your progress. Each group member can choose suggestions that will help him take the first steps toward change.

▶ 9. *The "Back Pages" Resources.* Be sure to check out the *Group Strengtheners* provided in the back pages of this book. You'll find: *Creative Session Starters*, a *Fellowship Day Idea Starter*, a *Video Night Discussion Outline*, and a *Prayer Record*.

So, ready to begin? Call the men, set a time and a place for your weekly meetings, and get started!

SESSION 1

*Dedicated...
or Just Busy?*

CHECK-IN/UPDATE

What's happening with you?

- A feeling to report
- A problem to share
- A personal or spiritual growth question or insight
- A summary of your week: issues, concerns, and joys
- A progress report or accountability check

▶ ONE MAN'S STORY

I had a good visit with one of America's most successful businessmen on a cross-country flight recently. He has risen from a very humble background to immense wealth. I asked him the secret of his success. His response was very interesting.

"Shrewdness!" was his one-word reply.

I was shocked by his frankness.

He went on to say that he spent every waking hour thinking, scheming, planning, developing, and putting deals together. In it all he had tried to be completely honest in all his affairs!

I couldn't help but admire his single-mindedness. He knew what he wanted and left nothing to chance. He worked hard to achieve his goals. All the power of his intellect, the strength of his seemingly limitless energies, the determination of his iron will, and the resources of his calculated discernment of people were employed to accomplish his goals.

When it seemed natural and unforced, I shifted our conversation into what the man believed about God.

There was a long silence. He admitted that he had not taken any time to think about that. He was astonished by my response: "If you ever put the same time, energy, and will into being a disciple of Jesus Christ, you would be a contemporary Apostle Paul."

The man's response was thoughtful and reflective: "Nobody has ever challenged me with that!"

The conversation with my traveling companion made a deep impression on me. It forced me to wonder if I could say that Jesus Christ meant as much to me as this man's career does to him. . . .

[Of course] Jesus commended shrewdness: "The sons of this age are more shrewd in relation to their own kind than the sons of light" (Luke 16:8). . . . He admired forthrightness, energetic planning, and complete devotion to a purpose. There is nothing wrong with creative strategizing. But it's alarming that people who make no pretense of knowing and loving God are more dedicated to the multiplication of their resources than the people of God are about the cause of spreading the Gospel and about the kingdom.

—Lloyd John Ogilvie[1]

▶ God Enters the Story

The LORD God took the man and put him in the Garden of Eden to work it and take care of it.
—*Genesis 2:15*

Jesus told His disciples: "There was a rich man whose manager was accused of wasting his possessions. So he called him in and asked him, 'What is this I hear about you? Give an account of your management, because you cannot be manager any longer.'

"The manager said to himself, 'What shall I do now? My master is taking away my job. I'm not strong enough to dig, and I'm ashamed to beg—I know what I'll do so that, when I lose my job here, people will welcome me into their houses.'

"So he called in each one of his master's debtors. He asked the first, 'How much do you owe my master?'

" 'Eight hundred gallons of olive oil,' he replied.

"The manager told him, 'Take your bill, sit down quickly, and make it four hundred.'

"Then he asked the second, 'And how much do you owe?'

" 'A thousand bushels of wheat,' he replied.

"He told him, 'Take your bill and make it eight hundred.'

"The master commended the dishonest manager because he had acted shrewdly. For the people of this world are more shrewd in dealing with their own kind than are the people of the light."
—*Luke 16:1-8*

Job and Career: Men at Work

No servant can serve two masters. Either he will hate the one and love the other, or he will be devoted to the one and despise the other. You cannot serve both God and Money.
—Luke 16:13

▶ The Story in Quotes

Why would a loving God put His children to work as soon as He created them? Because He knew human labor was a blessing. He knew it would provide them challenges, excitement, adventure, and rewards that nothing else would. He knew that creatures made in His image needed to devote their time to meaningful tasks.
—Bill Hybels[2]

Miss Woofenberg, our second-grade teacher, worked hard to instill a womanly view of manhood in us boys. She taught us that it was manly to be quiet and be nice.... She made us repress our urge to push ahead, to grab, to fight, to struggle, to press forward in man's relentless quest for superiority and world domination.

A man achieves world domination every time he does something awfully well. A guy who has a good fast ball, or knows physics like his own backyard, or can pick up a .22 and pick off a pine cone at a hundred yards knows this. Guys need this feeling if they're going to survive.... We have to be No. 1—sometime, somewhere, if only for ten minutes—or else we sag inside and become sad and careful, a guy who when he stands up you hear the tinkle of broken dreams.
—Garrison Keillor[3]

DEDICATED...OR JUST BUSY?

It is not enough to be busy; so are the ants. The question is: What are we busy about?
— Henry David Thoreau

▶ CAN YOU RELATE?

▶ Which one of the three story-sections above "rang a bell" with you? How?

▶ What personal story or experience comes to mind in relation to these themes:

(a) being aggressive and dedicated to the job
(b) feeling the tensions between career dedication and kingdom commitment

▶ What other insights came to the surface for you? What questions were raised in your mind? What personal applications are you considering?

▶ What else would you like to say about this topic?

▶ For Further Thought or Discussion

▶ In your opinion, is work primarily a "curse" as seen in Genesis 3:19 or a blessing as seen in Genesis 2:15? Why?

▶ What is happening when men begin to feel ashamed (around their families, or in a study course like this) about their drive to produce? Should we always assume that we are too dedicated to our careers? Explain.

▶ What does being "dedicated to the Gospel and the kingdom" mean for you, personally?

▶ How would you summarize the parable's "point" about shrewdness? What was Jesus trying to say to believers through this parable? (Read the full context in your Bible before answering.)

▶ How busy are you? To what extent are you busy for the "right" things? The "wrong" things? Explain.

▶ Everybody has to make a living and support his family. How do you relate this fact to Luke 16:13? What problems can arise in our priorities due to the fact that our working hours are much longer than the amount of time we spend worshiping or reading the Bible?

▶ What is your reaction to the quote by Garrison Keillor? Do you agree that the answer is *not* for men to become nicer, less driven by the desire to accomplish things and excel in their work? Explain.

▶ Prayer Moments

*S*pend some time going around the circle, naming specific prayer needs. Use the Prayer Record *on page 63 to jot notes. Then, choose a prayer method below.*

__ One man prays, covering issues and concerns raised.
__ Everyone prays for the man on his right.
__ Pray sentence prayers, with a person designated to close.
__ Focus on one key concern of the group or a group member, and all pray about that concern.
__ Spend some moments in silent prayer.
__ Assign specific prayer subjects to people before bowing for prayer.
__ Lay hands on a brother who expresses need, and focus on that man's situation.
__ Sing the doxology, or a praise chorus.
__ Other method:

▶ Suggestion for the Week Ahead

*F*or your devotional time this week, read and meditate on the Beatitudes found in Matthew 5:1-16.

Ask yourself: *How does Jesus' approach to life compare and contrast with my overall approach? With my drive to produce at work? Which of the Beatitudes speaks to me most clearly about adjusting my life style?*

What initial step could I take in order to become more aware of my true kingdom identity while on the job day by day?

SESSION 2

Success... or Failure?

CHECK-IN/UPDATE

What's happening with you?

- A feeling to report
- A problem to share
- A personal or spiritual growth question or insight
- A summary of your week: issues, concerns, and joys
- A progress report or accountability check

▶ ONE MAN'S STORY

A few years ago, I walked into my old junior high school to say hello to my mom, who was then serving as secretary to the principal. This was a surprise visit, and as soon as Mom saw me she called out to her boss: "Do you remember my son Gary, Mr. Munns?" The man did remember me from my student days, and he walked over for a handshake.

"Tell Mr. Munns what you're doing, Gary."

Responding to this invitation, I happily launched into a description of my duties as a bus driver for the Orange County Welfare Department, a job that had me carrying senior citizens and mental patients around to various government offices. It was my first real job out of college, and though it wasn't the greatest job, it was decent work, and I was content.

"No, Gary, tell him what you are *going* to be doing."

Yes, I had been formulating some plans to go to seminary and enter the ministry at some point... *but... what I am now isn't good enough, Mom? Isn't it good enough just to be your son, making an honest living?*

Of course, I sensed that she must have been proud of me, or she wouldn't have been so eager to reintroduce me to my old principal. But I also felt that she was a bit ashamed of me too—of my station in life at that point, anyway. To this day such remembered scenes move me onto old, well-worn paths of mental self-torture: *Have I been a failure so far? Will I ever come to a place of peace about where I am in life? Why do I never feel as though I've done enough?*

I think that, no matter how old we are, we will always long for our parents' complete approval—whether or not they are still alive. I know I often try to salve that longing by mentally toting up my career accomplishments, imagining how they might stand up in the court of parental opinion. Probably my own children are beginning to do the same thing. Certainly workaholics thrive on this raging inner quest for acceptance.

One man I know put it this way: "I wish I could have just once heard these words from my father, 'Son, I'm so very proud of you.' I think then I could have learned to relax a little in life; sit back and enjoy the ride a little more."

—Gary Wilde

▶ God Enters the Story

Then Jesus came from Galilee to the Jordan to be baptized by John. But John tried to deter Him, saying, "I need to be baptized by You, and do You come to me?"

Jesus replied, "Let it be so now; it is proper for us to do this to fulfill all righteousness. . . ."

As soon as Jesus was baptized, He went up out of the water. At that moment heaven was opened, and He saw the Spirit of God descending like a dove and lighting on Him. And a voice from heaven said, "This is my Son, whom I love; with Him I am well pleased."

—*Matthew 3:13-17*

Meanwhile His disciples urged Him, "Rabbi, eat something." But He said to them, "I have food to eat that you know nothing about."

Then His disciples said to each other, "Could someone have brought Him food?"

"My food," said Jesus, "is to do the will of Him who sent Me and to finish His work."

—*John 4:31-34*

Serve wholeheartedly, as if you were serving the Lord, not men, because you know that the Lord will reward everyone for whatever good he does, whether he is slave or free.

—*Ephesians 6:7-8*

▶ The Story in Quotes

"What happened to your father?"

"He never made it as a ballplayer, so

he tried to get his son to make it for him. By the time I was ten, playing baseball got to be like eating vegetables or taking out the garbage. So when I was fourteen, I started to refuse. Can you believe that? An American boy refusing to have a catch with his father? Anyway, when I was seventeen, I packed my things, said something awful, and left.

"After a while I wanted to come home, but I didn't know how.... Made it back for the funeral, though. The [man] died before I could tell him ... you know."

—Kevin Kostner, as Ray Kinsella, in the movie *Field of Dreams*

There are all different kinds of voices calling you to all different kinds of work, and the problem is to find out which is the voice of God rather than of Society, say, or the Superego, or Self-Interest.

By and large a good rule for finding out is this: The kind of work God usually calls you to is the kind of work (a) that you need most to do and (b) that the world most needs to have done. If you really get a kick out of your work, you've presumably met requirement (a), but if your work is writing cigarette ads, the chances are you've missed requirement (b).

—Frederick Buechner[4]

▶ Can You Relate?

▶ Which one of the three story-sections above "rang a bell" with you? How?

▶ What personal story or experience comes to mind, in relation to these themes:

(a) wanting parental approval

(b) struggling with feelings of failure

▸ What other insights came to the surface for you? What questions were raised in your mind? What personal applications are you considering?

▸ What else would you like to say about this topic?

▸ For Further Thought or Discussion

▸ Do you agree that we always long for our parents' approval? What is your own experience with that?

▸ At what point in your life were you most concerned with success and failure? How have you dealt with any doubts about your "success"?

▸ In what ways would the words of His Heavenly Father in Matthew 3:17 have helped prepare Jesus for His coming mission on earth? Do you have a solid sense of your own father's pride in you? Why, or why not?

▸ Discuss with a partner: When have you felt most like a "failure"? What objective facts and subjective feelings came into play? How would God have viewed you at that time?

▸ Did you ever sense that your parents were trying to live out their dreams through your life? Explain. Or: Do you have any indications that you have tried to do the same with your own children?

▸ Study the quote by Frederick Buechner. When have you struggled most with decisions about career choices and directions? What "voices" did you hear calling out to you? In light of Beuchner's two criteria, how would you rate your vocational choices so far?

▶ Prayer Moments

Spend some time going around the circle, naming specific prayer needs. Use the Prayer Record *on page 63 to jot notes. Then, choose a prayer method below.*

_ One man prays, covering issues and concerns raised.
_ Everyone prays for the man on his right.
_ Pray sentence prayers, with a person designated to close.
_ Focus on one key concern of the group or a group member, and all pray about that concern.
_ Spend some moments in silent prayer.
_ Assign specific prayer subjects to people before bowing for prayer.
_ Lay hands on a brother who expresses need, and focus on that man's situation.
_ Sing the doxology, or a praise chorus.

▶ Suggestion for the Week Ahead

In your journal, write your definition of success in life. Give this plenty of thought, and then think back over your life so far. Determine the extent your dreams and goals have been motivated by the values that come through in your definition.

Think:
▶ What do I *say* that I value the most in life?
▶ In light of how I have lived so far, what do I *demonstrate* as key values for me?
▶ What first step could I take to bring my *expressed values* and my *lived values* more in line?

SESSION 3

*Fame...
or Family?*

CHECK-IN/UPDATE

What's happening with you?

- A feeling to report
- A problem to share
- A personal or spiritual growth question or insight
- A summary of your week: issues, concerns, and joys
- A progress report or accountability check

▶ ONE MAN'S STORY

I love to sing. I have sung leading roles in a few operas and soloed professionally in oratorios and in church choirs. One day a voice teacher told me, "You have a beautiful voice—if you work with me, I know you will be doing major solos in the oratorio circuit in Chicago within two years."

I was ecstatic. I drove away, singing an aria from *Rigoletto* at the top of my lungs. I would build a career in voice! It would mean being gone four or five evenings a week, plus Saturdays and Sundays. But I could do it!

Then I saw in my mind the faces of our three children. Up to that point, my wife Juanita and I had made a commitment to be with them while they were growing up. I left work on time most days so I could help Lori complete her butter-tub miniature golf course in the back yard, or take Reyna on a bike ride, or go sledding with Joanna. But how could I be with the kids if I was away in the city every night of the week singing? How would I instruct, praise, and encourage them? *Yet, Lord, don't You want me to develop the talent with which You have so clearly gifted me?*

That night, I made the decision to give up singing at a competitive level—so I could be with my wife and our children. Yet to this day I think about it. Maybe I should have gone for it—followed my dream. Maybe if I had, I'd be famous.

I'm not saying I was a perfect father, either. But not long ago, I received a letter from Joanna, who has grown up and is living on her own now. She wrote, "I thank you for raising me to believe I have valuable resources within me. I really feel I can do anything. This is a gift I am eternally grateful for, and I know I am blessed to have been given such a father. I love you. Joanna."

—Larry Brook

▶ GOD ENTERS THE STORY

It will be like a man going on a journey, who called his servants and entrusted his property to them. To one he gave five talents of money, to another two talents, and to another one talent, each according to his ability. Then he went on his journey. The man who had received the five talents went at once and put his money to work and gained five more. So also, the one with the two talents gained two more. But the man who had received the one talent went off, dug a hole in the ground, and hid his master's money.

After a long time the master of those servants returned and settled accounts with them. . . . Then the man who had received the one talent came. "Master," he said, "I knew that you are a hard man, harvesting where you have not sown and gathering where you have not scattered seed. So I was afraid and went out and hid your talent in the ground. See, here is what belongs to you."

His master replied, "You wicked, lazy servant!"
—*Matthew 25:14-19, 24-26a*

Make it your ambition to lead a quiet life, to mind your own business and to work with your hands, just as we told you, so that your daily life may win the respect of outsiders and so that you will not be dependent on anybody.
—*1 Thessalonians 4:11-12*

Be imitators of God, therefore, as dearly loved children and live a life of love, just as Christ loved us and gave Himself up for us as a fragrant offering and sacrifice to God.
—*Ephesians 5:1-2*

▶ THE STORY IN QUOTES

To be a successful father there's one absolute rule: When you have a kid, don't look at it for the first two years.
—Ernest Hemingway[5]

Whenever I tried to talk about my family, I got all choked up. My four sons drank too much because of me. When they were growing up, I was too busy to play catch in the backyard. But when they were old enough to drink, we became drinking buddies. My kids have never blamed me. They don't have to. I blame myself. . . . I'm going to spend more time with all of them [now]—show them and tell them I love them.
—Mickey Mantle[6]

Each of us can change our own little world. Fathers who are honest with themselves will admit that we all make mistakes. We have all made bad decisions. Some of those decisions have to be reversed. If you have accepted a promotion and a transfer that takes you a step up the corporate ladder at the expense of your kids, maybe you need to think about taking a step back. More important than providing a life of ease for your kids is making sure they know you love them unconditionally.
—Mike Singletary[7]

Follow your bliss.
—Joseph Campbell[8]

▶ Can You Relate?

▶ Which one of the three story-sections above "rang a bell" with you? How?

▶ What personal story or experience comes to mind, in relation to these themes:

(a) giving up a dream or career goal because of family needs

(b) accomplishing a career goal, despite obstacles

- What other insights came to the surface for you? What questions were raised in your mind? What personal applications are you considering?
- What else would you like to say about this topic?

▶ For Further Thought or Discussion

- In what ways can you relate to Larry's story? In your opinion, did Larry make the right decision? What other options might he have chosen? What would you have done?
- How do you balance the call to develop your gifts (reach your vocational potential) and the seemingly competing call to be more of a "family man"?
- Joseph Campbell says that you should "follow your bliss" in life. What do you think this means? Do you agree, or disagree?
- Ephesians 5:1-2 calls us to a life that involves loving sacrifice, based on the example of Jesus. (See also Philippians 2:5-7.) How do you apply this principle to the "balancing act" between career goals and commitment to family?
- Do you have a sense that you are/were loved unconditionally by your parents? If you are a father, in what ways do you attempt to convey this kind of love?

▶ Prayer Moments

Spend some time going around the circle, naming specific prayer neeeds. Use the Prayer Record *on page 63 to jot notes. Then, choose a prayer method.*

Job and Career: Men at Work

— One man prays, covering issues and concerns raised.
— Everyone prays for the man on his right.
— Pray sentence prayers, with a person designated to close.
— Focus on one key concern of the group or a group member, and all pray about that concern.
— Spend some moments in silent prayer.
— Assign specific prayer subjects to people before bowing for prayer.
— Lay hands on a brother who expresses need, and focus on that man's situation.
— Sing the doxology, or a praise chorus.
— Other method:

▶ Suggestion for the Week Ahead

Dig out the last performance review you received at work. Or read through your work goals (sales quota, or project objectives) for the coming year. Contact someone that you trust, perhaps a friend from your group, to go over these with you. Together, analyze your skill at balancing work and family demands. Discuss:

▸ How realistic is my manager in asking me to accomplish these things?
▸ How much time and energy will/have these kinds of goals require(d) of me?
▸ How well have I been able to reserve time and energy for my family while pursuing these standards at work?
▸ What legitimate adjustments to my "drive to produce" might I consider?

SESSION 4

Quit... or Stick with It?

CHECK-IN/UPDATE

What's happening with you?

- A feeling to report
- A problem to share
- A personal or spiritual growth question or insight
- A summary of your week: issues, concerns, and joys
- A progress report or accountability check

▶ ONE MAN'S STORY

After staring at the phone for a whole minute, I pushed my chair back from my desk, took a sip of coffee and wondered, *Why am I even thinking about this?*

When I started working in my job nine years ago I had many hopes, dreams, and goals. And yet after numerous project successes, promotions, and increased responsibilities, I'm considering another job that will launch me in a whole new direction. I know I can stay here in the relative stability and security of a job I've mastered—and perhaps feel a little bored once in a while—or risk a career change and start investing my time and energy elsewhere.

As I sit in my office and mull it over, I can come up with some nice-sounding reasons to consider a change. Because of the birth of our first child, I must plan wisely for the future. My wife doesn't work outside the home, and this job has limited financial potential. Will it be enough over the long haul?

Then there's my desire to use my talents and abilities to their fullest potential. Am I really still challenged by this work? Or am I at the point of being held back from personal development? Will a career change give me the opportunity to fully develop my skills?

There's also the fact that I feel a bit taken for granted here. The hassles of overwork and lack of gratitude are starting to get to me. Is it just me? Do I need to adjust my attitude? Or am I really starting to experience some abuse here?

It's certainly difficult to think about leaving; change is scary, and failure is a definite possibility. I've invested nine years in this company, in its products, and in my relationships with coworkers. I've been through both the good times and the bad with this company. And I've stayed because I believe in the company and what it does.

As I struggle with these issues, I've come to at least one clear conclusion, though: my work does matter to God. Just knowing that fact, however, doesn't give me the answer to the crucial question facing me right now: Should I pick up this phone and say to the recruiter, "Yes, I'm ready to make a move"? Or should I suck it up and keep hanging in there?

—Troy Reichert

▶ God Enters the Story

When I surveyed all that my hands had done and what I had toiled to achieve, everything was meaningless, a chasing after the wind; nothing was gained under the sun.

Then I turned my thoughts to consider wisdom, and also madness and folly. What more can the king's successor do than what has already been done? I saw that wisdom is better than folly, just as light is better than darkness. The wise man has eyes in his head, while the fool walks in the darkness; but I came to realize that the same fate overtakes them both.

Then I thought in my heart, "The fate of the fool will overtake me also. What then do I gain by being wise?" I said in my heart, "This too is meaningless." For the wise man, like the fool, will not be long remembered; in days to come both will be forgotten. Like the fool, the wise man too must die!

So I hated life, because the work that is done under the sun was grievous to me. All of it is meaningless, a chasing after the wind. I hated all the things I had toiled for under the sun, because I must leave them to the one who comes after me. And who knows whether he will be a wise man or a fool? Yet he will have control over all the work into which I have poured my effort and skill under the sun. This too is meaningless.

So my heart began to despair over all my toilsome labor under the sun. For a man may do his work with wisdom, knowledge and skill, and then he must leave all he owns to someone who has not worked for it. This too is meaningless and a great misfortune. What does a man get for all the toil and

anxious striving with which he labors under the sun?
—*Ecclesiastes 2:11-22*

However, as it is written: "No eye has seen, no ear has heard, no mind has conceived what God has prepared for those who love Him."
—*1 Corinthians 2:9*

▶ THE STORY IN QUOTES

The reason I resigned at this time is because the duties and the pressures of this position have begun to make me into something that I don't want to be.
—Dan Issel, former head coach of the Denver Nuggets[9]

A young woman waits for fulfillment, stereotypically, by becoming engaged, by being in a relationship. But so, too, does a young man wait and crave to be engaged, to be in a relationship. Engaged in a career, that is in a relationship with work. Engaged: like a gear meshing smoothly, a productive and essential and well-cared-for part of the larger machine. It is in your work that you most often look to be recognized, embraced, wanted, identified, made to feel useful and productive, made to be someone. The things a woman wants from you, at least in the early years, you want from your job.
—James E. Dittes[10]

Women have often lamented that society judges them almost exclusively in terms of their bodies and looks, reducing them to "sex objects." Men are subject to even more impersonal standards; they tend to be judged by their career and salaries, standards which reduce them to "success objects."

Many men have so much of their identity invested in their jobs that when they are forced to retire, they die—because they see their life and value as inextricably entwined with what they do. How tragic, then, that so many men are trapped in stultifying jobs. Not even when they are at work can they find fulfillment.

—Christopher Harding[11]

▶ Can You Relate?

▶ Which one of the three story-sections above "rang a bell" with you? How?

▶ What personal story or experience comes to mind, in relation to these themes:

(a) feeling bored or unappreciated at work

(b) struggling with a career-change decision

▶ What other insights came to the surface for you? What questions were raised in your mind? Do you have any personal applications to consider?

▶ What else would you like to say about this topic?

▶ For Further Thought or Discussion

▶ What would you do, if you were Troy? Why?

▶ When have you been bored with your job? How do you weigh the benefit of stability with the risk of making a career change in a situation like Troy's?

What are the pros and cons of "hanging in there"? Give an example, if possible.

▸ Are you convinced that your own work "matters to God"? Explain.

▸ How can the promises of Scripture in 1 Corinthians 2:9 help us get through the tough, boring times on the job described in Ecclesiastes 2:11-22?

▸ Look at the quote by coach Dan Issel. How have the duties and pressures of your own jobs shaped your personality over the years? Do you like what you are becoming as a result? Explain.

▸ Do you agree that "the things a woman wants from you . . . you want from your job"? Tell about times when you felt "recognized, embraced, wanted, identified, useful, and productive" because of your work. When that isn't happening at work, how do you meet your needs for those things?

▸ Prayer Moments

Spend time going around the circle, naming specific prayer needs. Use the Prayer Record *on page 63 to jot notes. Then, choose a prayer method below.*

__ One man prays, covering issues and concerns raised.
__ Everyone prays for the man on his right.
__ Pray sentence prayers, with a person designated to close.
__ Focus on one key concern of the group or a group member, and all pray about that concern.
__ Spend some moments in silent prayer.
__ Assign prayer subjects to people before bowing for prayer.

— Lay hands on a brother who expresses need, and focus on that man's situation.
— Sing the doxology, or a praise chorus.
— Other method:

▶ Suggestion for the Week Ahead

Take some time this week to evaluate the career choice you've made (no matter what age you are). During a period of silence, think back to times when you felt highly engaged, energized, refreshed, inspired, or exhilarated by a project that you have done in any of your past jobs. This may have taken place in an informal work setting, or for a church committee, for a volunteer organization, or just on your own.

Ask yourself: *What talents or skills did this project tap into? What are the abilities that I thoroughly enjoyed using in this work? To what extent does my present employment allow me to use these talents, skills, and abilities? What alternative career or profession might make better use of who I am?*

If you are motivated to check out the possibilities of another career, try to talk to a man in that career path (perhaps at your church) who can tell you more about the day-to-day characteristics of his job.

SESSION 5

Knuckle Under... or Blow the Whistle?

CHECK-IN/UPDATE

What's happening with you?

- A feeling to report
- A problem to share
- A personal or spiritual growth question or insight
- A summary of your week: issues, concerns, and joys
- A progress report or accountability check

▶ ONE MAN'S STORY

"Because we're not making sales goals," came the answer, one long and particularly late afternoon. And as I walked away from the meeting I really couldn't believe what I had just heard. I was caught in the middle. My conscience said this wasn't right, and yet the vice president of our division was ordering me to execute a questionable plan to close out the final month of our fiscal year. The plan was at best on the borderline of being ethical, at worst downright dishonest.

Working in a Christian organization can be both a blessing and a curse. And the longer I worked in the corporate headquarters, the more I saw the dark side. I came to realize the ethical dilemma that I had been drawn into. We had a rich heritage of serving Christians, yet I saw the erosion of our reputation as corporate decisions began succumbing to selfish motives. And when push came to shove, I could see the customer getting trampled in the process.

The part that troubled me most was the way these business decisions were couched in the cloak of Christian good will. "This is what is best for the customer" was the standard mantra, even though we were forcing product into our channels of distribution that stores had never ordered.

I faced many tough questions about myself and about the leadership of the company. At times I doubted my abilities and my courage: *If I don't do something about this, who will stand up for what is right?* Yet I needed this job to take care of my family. If I stood up against the vice president, I would either be fired or labeled a troublemaker. Simply leaving was a tremendous risk that I couldn't afford. But being shuffled off to the management sidelines wasn't a pleasant prospect either.

Through everything, I've wondered about my faith. If I really had faith that God would provide, I wouldn't worry about my job or my reputation, would I? I'd stand up for what was ethical, and just let the chips fall where they may, right?

—Name withheld by request

▶ GOD ENTERS THE STORY

"What shall I give you?" [Laban] asked.
"Don't give me anything," Jacob replied. "But if you will do this one thing for me, I

will go on tending your flocks and watching over them: Let me go through all your flocks today and remove from them every speckled or spotted sheep, every dark-colored lamb and every spotted or speckled goat. They will be my wages. And my honesty will testify for me in the future, whenever you check on the wages you have paid me. Any goat in my possession that is not speckled or spotted, or any lamb that is not dark-colored, will be considered stolen."

"Agreed," said Laban. "Let it be as you have said. . . ."

Jacob, however, took fresh-cut branches from poplar, almond and plane trees and made white stripes on them by peeling the bark and exposing the white inner wood of the branches. Then he placed the peeled branches in all the watering troughs, so that they would be directly in front of the flocks when they came to drink. When the flocks were in heat and came to drink, they mated in front of the branches. And they bore young that were streaked or speckled or spotted. Jacob set apart the young of the flock by themselves. . . . Thus he made separate flocks for himself and did not put them with Laban's animals. Whenever the stronger females were in heat, Jacob would place the branches in the troughs in front of the animals so they would mate near the branches, but if the animals were weak, he would not place them there. So the weak animals went to Laban and the strong ones to Jacob. In this way the man grew exceedingly prosperous and came to own large flocks, and maidservants and menservants, and camels and donkeys.

—*Genesis 30:31-34, 37-43*

The man of integrity walks securely, but he who takes crooked paths will be found out.
—*Proverbs 10:9*

▶ THE STORY IN QUOTES

Greed is all right.... Greed is healthy. You can be greedy and still feel good about yourself.
—Ivan Boesky[12]

Most of us can easily discern that falsifying tax records or pilfering supplies is wrong. But so many issues of integrity in the workplace are gray areas, in which the line between right and wrong is blurred. Is it altogether right, for example, to enthusiastically recommend someone for employment when you know of serious questions regarding that person's competence? Is it right to use your influence as a corporate executive to bump someone else off an overbooked flight and take his place yourself? ... Questions like these are matters of conscience. That means that there are no explicit biblical instructions one way or the other, and there are no legal statutes involved.
—Doug Sherman and William Hendricks[13]

Any time you commit to living a more godly life, you are entering enemy territory. Expect spiritual conflict. Whether it is fashionable or not, integrity involves a price, but the cost pales in comparison with the cost of compromise. People can ruin your reputation, but no one can take away your integrity.
—Paul Kroger[14]

JOB AND CAREER: MEN AT WORK

It's no trick to make a lot of money, if all you want to do is make a lot of money.
—Orson Welles, as Charles Foster Kane, in the movie *Citizen Kane*

And I couldn't have done it without God, my wife and family, and my laptop computer.

▶ Can You Relate?

▶ Which one of the three story-sections above "rang a bell" with you? How?

▶ What personal story or experience comes to mind, in relation to these themes:

(a) being aware of unethical practices at work

(b) deciding whether or not to "blow the whistle"

▶ What other insights came to the surface for you? What questions were raised in your mind? What personal applications are you considering?

▶ What else would you like to say about this topic?

▶ For Further Thought or Discussion

▶ How do you answer the storyteller's two questions (in the last paragraph of One Man's Story)?

▶ What ethical challenges have you encountered in your workplace? How have you dealt with them?

▶ Do you agree with the statement that sometimes "there are no explicit biblical instructions one way or the other"? If so, what is a Christian man's recourse in such situations?

▶ Jacob obviously fooled Laban by deceitfully altering his "wages." Why would God allow Jacob to get away with this? To what extent do you believe a Christian man can keep following a questionable course without paying a consequence?

▶ Do you "expect spiritual conflict" when you commit to ethical dealings at work? When have you experienced such conflict?

▶ What did Paul Kroger mean by his statement: "People can ruin your reputation, but no one can take away your integrity"? Give a practical example of how this fact plays into a man's ethical decision-making at work.

▶ Prayer Moments

Spend some time going around the circle, naming specific requests. Use the Prayer Record *on page 63 to jot notes. Then, choose a prayer method below.*

__ One man prays, covering issues and concerns raised.
__ Everyone prays for the man on his right.
__ Pray sentence prayers, with a person designated to close.
__ Focus on one key concern of the group or a group member, and all pray about that concern.
__ Spend some moments in silent prayer.
__ Assign specific prayer subjects to people before bowing for prayer.
__ Lay hands on a brother who expresses need, and focus on that man's situation.
__ Sing the doxology, or a praise chorus.

▶ Suggestion for the Week Ahead

For your devotional time this week, consider reading through the whole chapter of Micah 6. Notice how seriously God takes ethical dealings among His people. Notice also the severe judgment God promises to those who seek to gain at the expense of others.

Think: *Have I ever felt the kind of futility described in 6:14?* If so, reexamine your business and personal dealings to see if they are completely ethical.

SESSION 6

Contentment... or "Life Engineering"?

CHECK-IN/UPDATE

What's happening with you?

- A feeling to report
- A problem to share
- A personal or spiritual growth question or insight
- A summary of your week: issues, concerns, and joys
- A progress report or accountability check

▶ ONE MAN'S STORY

Not too long ago, I went to my mailbox and pulled out one of those chain letters that promises a load of cash flowing my way if only I'll send my name on to the next person in line (along with a ten-dollar bill). The purely rational side of me knows that those letters are scams, but they still appeal to another part of me that hopes to suddenly latch onto a sure thing.

I call this compulsive desire my Ralph Cramden Complex. I'm secretly on the lookout for the "big win," the idea or the plan that will earn me a quick buck—maybe even a small fortune. Poor Ralph kept trying, but his little schemes always backfired. It only took him a half-hour of "The Honeymooners" TV show each week to realize that he couldn't force things to turn out exactly the way he wanted them. Always, at the end of the show, he had to admit that his attempts to engineer his future only served to make him look rather foolish.

It's the same with me. On the one hand, I am constantly hit with new schemes that pull at me to take control of my life, to work everything out the way I want it. There is no end of voices telling me that I can run my own life if I'll just sign on the dotted line and send in a little deposit up front. Yet another voice is calling out to me too. It is the voice of the Spirit who lives within me, telling me that I can rest in the hands of One who guarantees no security in this life, because He has a home waiting for me that is not of this world. He tells me I must not become too attached to the imperfect here, lest I lose sight of the perfect future He has in store for me. So He tells me to learn contentment.

It's a tough call. The first approach requires "life engineering"—trying to force events to be the way I want them (with no guarantee against constant frustration). The second approach calls me to a trusting openness to life's way of bringing what is beyond my shabby expectations. And really, can I ever do this: create a world of satisfaction for myself, rather than receive my happiness as a gift?

—Gary Wilde

▶ GOD ENTERS THE STORY

I rejoice greatly in the Lord that at last you have renewed your concern for me.

Indeed, you have been concerned, but you had no opportunity to show it. I am not saying this because I am in need, for I have learned to be content whatever the circumstances. I know what it is to be in need, and I know what it is to have plenty. I have learned the secret of being content in any and every situation, whether well fed or hungry, whether living in plenty or in want. I can do everything through him who gives me strength.

Yet it was good of you to share in my troubles.
— *Philippians 4:10-14*

▶ THE STORY IN QUOTES

Because we lack a divine Center, our need for security has led us into an insane attachment to things. We must clearly understand that the lust for affluence in contemporary society is psychotic. It is psychotic because it has completely lost touch with reality. We crave things we neither need nor enjoy. We buy things we do not want to impress people we do not like. . . . Covetousness we call ambition. Hoarding we call prudence. Greed we call industry.

— Richard Foster[15]

The Christian doctrine of suffering explains, I believe, a very curious fact about the world we live in. The settled happiness and security which we all desire, God withholds from us by the very nature of the world: but joy, pleasure, and merriment He has scattered broadcast. We are never safe, but we have plenty of fun, and some ecstasy. It is not hard to see why. The security we crave would teach us to rest our hearts in this world and oppose an obstacle to our return to God: a few moments of happy love, a landscape, a symphony, a merry meeting with our friends, a bath or a football match, have no such tendency. Our Father refreshes us on the journey with some pleasant inns, but will not encourage us to mistake them for home.

—C.S. Lewis[16]

It's an old adage that the way to be safe is never to be secure.... Each one of us requires the spur of insecurity to force us to do our best.

—Harold W. Dodds

▶ Can You Relate?

▶ Which one of the three sections "rang a bell" with you? How?

▶ What personal story or experience comes to mind, in relation to these themes:

(a) the idea of "life engineering"

(b) the idea of learning contentment in a world bent on hoarding

▶ What other insights came to the surface for you? What questions were raised in your mind? What personal applications are you considering?

▶ What else would you like to say about this topic?

▶ For Further Thought or Discussion

▶ When are you most tempted to "scheme" your way through a situation? How does that usually work out?

▶ How hard or easy is it for you to trust God with

your happiness? What does it actually mean for a man to "give up control" of his life?

▸ How can we maintain our enthusiasm and energy for earning a living and still live by grace, receiving our lives as a gift?

▸ How do Paul's statements about contentment help you—or complicate the issue for you?

▸ How would your life have to change in order for you to be able to say: "I am content"? or "I can do all things through Christ"? Describe that kind of life, in practical terms, using your particular work and family situation.

▸ What would it mean for you, personally, to become less "attached" to things, and to control?

▸ Prayer Moments

Spend some time going around the circle, naming specific requests. Use the Prayer Record *on page 63 to jot notes. Then, choose a prayer method below.*

__ One man prays, covering issues and concerns raised.
__ Everyone prays for the man on his right.
__ Pray sentence prayers, with a person designated to close.
__ Focus on one key concern of the group or a group member, and all pray about that concern.
__ Spend some moments in silent prayer.
__ Assign specific prayer subjects to people before bowing for prayer.
__ Lay hands on a brother who expresses need, and focus on that man's situation.
__ Sing the doxology, or a praise chorus.

▶ Suggestion for the Week Ahead

If you are married, consider raising this topic with your wife this week. Talk about a way you have tried to "engineer" your life in the past. Discuss together how this has affected your relationship. What changes might help?

During a "quiet time" this week, open yourself to a new level of trust in Christ's good will toward you—and His provision for you. In silence, wait before Him.

Group Strengtheners

Draw on the following resources to deepen the fellowship in your group, both in the meeting and during the week.

CREATIVE SESSION STARTERS

Here are some creative ideas to help you launch into the topic of each session. For some sessions you'll just immediately start with discussion, but other times you may want to plan ahead and prepare to use one of these more active starter ideas. A few days in advance, read through the suggestion for your week to see if it would spark interest and discussion in your group. Feel free to adapt the ideas to your own group's size and setting. It's your call.

For Session 1

If your group is new, and many of the men do not know each other, you may wish to start with this icebreaker activity. Tell everyone that you are going to give them a brief amount of time just to "mingle" before the session begins. Here are the instructions for these mingle-moments: Each man must talk with at least three other men for no longer than one minute each. During these three quickie conversations, each man must tell about "the two most important things to know about me."

When everyone has mingled, ask for introductions by having each man talk about one of the other men's "important" qualities. When the introductions are complete, discuss:

- ▸ To what extent were your conversations focused on job and vocation?
- ▸ In most situations of meeting other men, how long does it typically take for the conversation to get around to: "And what do you do for a living"?
- ▸ In your opinion, is the question about your "vocational identity" something you enjoy discussing, or would you rather avoid it? Why?

Make your transition to the session theme by pointing out that in this session you'll be exploring together the drive to produce and accomplish in our jobs—and how to balance that drive to excel with a wise consideration of the goals for which we use our God-given energy.

For Session 2

Start this session by gathering the men in a circle and asking everyone to close their eyes for a few moments. Stand outside the circle and say: "Imagine that I am your father. (Silence) I am going to be placing my hands on your shoulders, but it is really your own father's hands. (Silence)

Go around the circle, standing behind each man, placing your hands firmly on the shoulders of each. Say to each: "(Name), I'm so very proud of you." Allow plenty of silence in order to let the statement have impact. When you have gone around the circle, invite reactions to the exercise. Ask:

- When did you experience this type of affirmation from your father? Describe the event.
- When did you wish this had happened?
- What sense of either satisfaction or longing do you still have related to your father's (or mother's) approval?

Move into the session by pointing out that feelings of success or failure may be tied to our sense of acceptance in the eyes of our parents. Invite everyone to join in that discussion.

For Session 3

Distribute one index card to each man. Invite the men to think about any important decision they've made in life, or a turning point they've reached where they've chosen one path over another. Ask them to jot a brief description of an "If Only": What their life might be like now if they had made the *other* choice—the competing decision or the alternative path.

When everyone has an *If Only* description jotted down, gather the cards in a small container, shuffle them, and read them aloud. Have some fun guessing who wrote what.

Then discuss:

- What is it like for you when you give up on a goal or a dream because of family needs?
- Has this usually been a decision that turned out "for the best" or "for the worst"? Why?

Move into your session by remarking that you'll be looking closely at the tension we feel when faced with a choice between pursuing our vocational dreams and wanting to be at home with family.

For Session 4
Divide into two groups by asking the men: Who has quit something in their lives (a sports team, a committee, a job, other)? Who has never (or almost never) quit anything?

Have the Quitters sit together, and then hand each of them a construction-paper-and-string necklace to wear that has the word QUITTER written on it in bold letters. (Note: It's okay if everyone in your group is a Quitter. Just ask the first set of questions below.) Ask:

To the Quitters:
- Why did you quit? What are the pros and cons of quitting?
- How much internal or external pressure did you feel to conform to the "manly" idea that you should "never give up"?

To the Non-Quitters (if there are any):
- Do you look down on those Quitters a bit? Explain.
- In what ways has "hanging in there" helped you or your family? Hurt you or your family?

After brief discussion, move into your study time.

For Session 5
Gather everyone in a circle and tell the men that you are going to read a series of situations that may or may not be ethical. Their task is to decide.

Hand a small whistle to the man on your right. Let everyone know that the way each man (in turn) will respond to his situation after it is read will be to either blow the whistle or put his body into a posture that indicates: "I'd knuckle under to this."

After each response (whistle, or knuckle under) have the man tell why he responded as he did. Here are the situations (add your own, depending on the size of your group):

▸ Your boss asks you to take an important client to a show that features a "Wet T-Shirt Contest."
▸ You notice that your foreman has used untreated lumber in the bathroom framing of a house you are building.
▸ You receive $5.00 extra on your paycheck this week, for no apparent reason.
▸ Your female boss keeps telling you dirty jokes.
▸ You've just been passed over for a promotion, apparently because of your race.
▸ You notice a fellow worker leaving early several days in a row.

Allow for brief discussion, then begin your session.

For Session 6
Focus attention on the concept of "life engineering." Hand everyone an index card and invite the men to

write two very brief personal obituaries. On one side of the card should be written: *How your life turned out, assuming you had complete control of it and could have made everything work out just as you wanted it to be.* On the other side of the card: *How you think your life will actually turn out, as you seek to give control of your life to God.*

When everyone is finished, invite volunteers to read their two imaginary obituaries. Ask them to explain any similarities or contrasts. Then discuss together: *To what extent are you truly convinced that God has the best in mind for you?*

Fellowship Day Idea Starter

A men's group can be more than just a weekly meeting. For the best results in deepening your fellowship, schedule outside activities at least once per quarter. Try doing a sports activity, or attending a special event together. With a little planning, you can make these outings into times of Christian fellowship.

This particular activity will take significant advance planning, but will be well worth the effort. Develop a plan together, with your work calendars, to schedule one or more "on-site visits" to one another's workplaces. The man being visited on a particular day could take some part of the day off (with advance permission from supervisors!) to show the others through his office, plant, warehouse, or project site, explaining exactly what he does for a living. Culminate the time with a lunch or dinner as a group.

Be creative with this. You could either work on trying to get everyone together for the visits, or just pair up and have partners schedule times when they could exchange visits and have lunch together. The point is to see one another in the context of work, rather than just relating at a weekly group meeting. If the visits are done before the study course begins, or during the weeks of your study, then your discussion times will become more relevant and practical. At any rate, the men will get to know each other—their work challenges and stresses, joys and disappointments—at a deeper level.

Video Night Discussion Outline

Here's a suggestion for a video to watch with your group at some time during the weeks of your focus on job and career. You may wish to use the video night as a way of launching your course, or you could use it as a post-course get-together. (Warning: This video contains an occasional coarse word. Preview it first to decide if it is appropriate for your particular group.)

Movie: *Mr. Mom*
- PG
- 90 minutes
- A 1983 film

What's It All About?
Mr. Mom is a comedy depicting the challenges a man faces when he is laid off from his job and has to spend his days at home with the kids. It's a lighthearted film, but through the dramatic technique of role reversal, it brings out key issues related to how a man feels about the value of his work and his role in the family.

JOB AND CAREER: MEN AT WORK

The Main Characters
- Jack: an engineer, laid off from an auto plant in Detroit
- Caroline: Jack's wife, a homemaker who becomes an advertising executive
- Ron: the ad agency supervisor, who makes passes at Caroline
- Neighbor woman (played by Ann Jillian) who makes passes at Jack
- Kenny, Megan, and Alex: Jack and Caroline's three children

The Plot in a Nutshell
Jack is happy in his work as an engineer at a Detroit auto factory. But early in the film he is called into the office by his boss and, along with two friends, laid off indefinitely.

He is at first excited about having some time off, confident that he will be able to find another position immediately. But a couple of weeks go by—and no job. Finally, Caroline suggests that she herself seek work. This bothers Jack, but he makes it into a competition: "I bet you a hundred to one that I'll get a job before you do."

He loses the bet, and Caroline goes to work full time, becoming quite successful. Jack stays at home to be a "house husband"—learning to cook the meals, clean the house, and change diapers.

General Discussion
Do you believe that men are really so out of touch with the chores of child-rearing and domestic duties? Why, or why not? Can you give a personal example? How exaggerated—or stereotyped—is Jack's apparent incompetence?

Is the point of the movie basically sexist? (Is it really saying, "Keep the little woman at home" or, "We all know that men do best as workers, not as caretakers"?)

Key Themes, Scenes, and Quotes
Your discussion may develop more specifically around any of these numbered themes:

▶ 1. *A man's apparent unfamiliarity with home duties and child-rearing.* In one scene, Caroline says to the kids as she leaves for her first day of work: "Take it easy on Daddy; he's a rookie."

Discuss: *Are you a family life "rookie"? How would you cope in Jack's situation as a rookie homemaker? Have you ever been in that situation? What happened?*

▶ 2. *A man's supposed need to be the "breadwinner" in the home.* Jack really lets himself go after awhile. He grows a beard and gains weight. He wears the same shirt, day after day. He sleeps in and lays around watching the soap operas on TV.

Caroline: "You're mad, aren't you?"

Jack: "I'm not mad. I'm just not where I want to be right now."

Discuss: *Are you more comfortable facing the challenges at work or the challenges of your relationships at home? Where do you most want to be? Why?*

▶ 3. *The depression that hits during a period of unemployment.*

Caroline: "Take a look at yourself. You've really thrown in the towel, honey."

Jack: "My brain is like oatmeal. I yelled at Kenny today for coloring outside the lines! Megan and I are starting to watch the same TV shows...and I'm I'm liking them! I'm losin' it!

Discuss: *If our identities are more than just what we do for a living, why do we become so devastated when our jobs are taken away?*

▶ 4. ***Men and women wanting some of the same things from each other in a family.*** Jack finds himself longing for more of his wife's presence and companionship at home—as so often happens, but in reverse.

Jack: "Even when you're here, you're not here."

Caroline: "What? You don't want me to succeed?"

Jack: "Of course I want you to succeed.... But it's real easy to forget what's important. So don't."

Discuss: *Have you ever had a conversation like this with your wife? If so, were you "Jack" or "Caroline"? How have you worked at resolving this conflict?*

▶ 5. ***The value of work in a man's life, and the identity and pride it provides.*** Jack is asked to do something unethical in order to have his old job back. He refuses, explaining the basic way he sees himself.

Jack: "I'm a car maker. I make cars. I take a lot of pride in my work."

Discuss: *What scriptural principles indicate to you that God wants us to find esteem and fulfillment through our work? How would you describe the limits of this type of fulfillment, in light of our calling as kingdom citizens?* (See Philippians 3:17-21.)

GROUP STRENGTHENERS

PRAYER RECORD

Spend some time sharing prayer concerns before closing your session in prayer together. Use this page to jot notes as others speak, then determine together the method you'll use to pray. Periodically review the record as a group to discover how prayers have been answered—or to receive updated information.

Name	Request/Concern/Praise

NOTES

1. Lloyd John Ogilvie, *The Autobiography of God* (Ventura, Calif.: Regal Books, 1979). Used by permission.
2. Bill Hybels, *Honest to God?* (Grand Rapids, Mich.: Zondervan, 1990).
3. Garrison Keillor, *The Book of Guys* (New York: Viking Press, 1993).
4. Frederick Buechner, *Wishful Thinking* (New York: HarperCollins, 1993).
5. Jon Winokur, *Friendly Advice* (New York: Dutton, 1990).
6. Mickey Mantle, after admitting himself into the Betty Ford alcoholic rehabilitation center. In *Sports Illustrated*, April 18, 1994.
7. Mike Singletary, *Singletary on Singletary* (Nashville: Thomas Nelson, 1991).
8. Joseph Campbell, *The Power of Myth* (New York: Doubleday, 1988).
9. WLS radio interview, Chicago, Ill., January, 1995.
10. James E. Dittes, *The Male Predicament: On Being a Man Today* (San Francisco: Harper and Row, 1985).
11. Christopher Harding, ed., *Wingspan: Inside the Men's Movement* (New York: St. Martin's Press, 1992).
12. Ivan Boesky in a commencement address at the University of California at Berkeley, May 18, 1986.
13. Doug Sherman and William Hendricks, *Your Work Matters to God* (Colorado Springs: NavPress, 1993).
14. Paul Kroger, "Integrity at Work" (article in *New Man* magazine, Nov./Dec., 1994).
15. Richard Foster, *Celebration of Discipline* (San Francisco: Harper and Row, 1978).
16. C.S. Lewis, *The Problem of Pain* (New York: Macmillan, 1962).